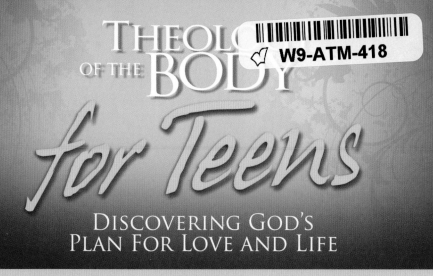

THEOLOGY OF THE BODY
for Teens
DISCOVERING GOD'S PLAN FOR LOVE AND LIFE

MIDDLE SCHOOL EDITION

Parent's Guide

Monica Ashour,
Brian Butler, Jason Evert,
and Colin & Aimee MacIver

ASCENSION

West Chester, Pennsylvania

Ascension
Post Office Box 1990
West Chester, PA 19380
1-800-376-0520
ascensionpress.com

Cover design: Devin Schadt

Printed in the United States of America

ISBN: 978-1-935940-07-4

CONTENTS

About the Authors

 Monica Ashour is co-founder and executive director of the Theology of the Body Evangelization Team (TOBET), a nonprofit group that promotes St. John Paul II's seminal work. She speaks nationally to teens and pre-teens on the gift of their sexuality and is dedicated to helping them transform their lives through an understanding of the Theology of the Body. Monica resides in Dallas, Texas.

 Brian Butler is the co-founder and president of Dumb Ox Ministries, a nonprofit organization dedicated to chastity and vocation formation for teens, pre-teens, and young adults. He is co-author of *Theology of the Body for Teens: High School* and *Middle School Editions.* He resides with his wife, Lisa, and their children in the New Orleans area.

 Jason Evert is a best-selling author of a dozen books, including *Theology of His/Her Body* and *How to Find Your Soulmate without Losing Your Soul.* He also co-authored *Theology of the Body for Teens: High School* and *Middle School Editions.* Jason has spoken internationally to more than a million teens and pre-teens about the virtue of chastity. He resides with his wife, Crystalina, and their children in Denver, Colorado.

 Aimee and Colin MacIver teach theology at Saint Scholastica Academy in Covington, Louisiana, where Colin serves as the religion department chair and campus ministry coordinator. In addition to teaching in Catholic high schools, they have also served in various youth ministries for nearly ten years. The MacIvers reside in the New Orleans area with their young son.

Introduction

R emember when you were in middle school? You probably looked in
the mirror twenty times a day. Most of us were wholly concerned
with ourselves—our looks, friends, popularity, "crushes," and even
boyfriends and girlfriends. It was a time of excitement and changes,
laced with anxiety and difficulties.

Today's middle schoolers, though, face new pressures. Social
networking, texting, online video gaming, and the whole gamut of
virtual reality present new horizons of connectivity, yet often without
real communion, adding to the hard task of early adolescents finding
their identity.

To be sure, the stakes are high for today's middle schoolers. Consider
the statistics regarding the psychosomatic development of adolescents.
Recent studies in neuroscience demonstrate that the growth and
maturation process of the adolescent brain continues well past age
eighteen.[1] Much of the development immediately prior to and during
puberty is in the frontal lobe, the area of the brain that controls
reasoning, planning, and impulse control.[2] Other studies show that the
parts of the brain that govern reward sensitivity are in high gear during
puberty, which can lead to an illogical pursuit of sensations even in
the face of risks.[3] Finally, there is also evidence that the brain systems
that process emotional and social information are greatly affected by
hormonal changes during puberty, making early adolescents more

sensitive to the reactions of those around them—and thus more susceptible to being adversely impacted by peer pressure.[4]

Add in the emotional roller coaster induced by hormones and society's virtual IV-drip of sex-saturated music and movies, and it is easy to see why it is so hard for today's adolescents to make good relationship decisions. For many parents, all of this seems to be a recipe for confusion and heartache. Some find themselves either unintentionally out of touch or paralyzed somewhere between fear and a sense of being overwhelmed. Because many parents themselves have faced the challenges of divorce, single parenting, raising grandchildren, and a variety of other family circumstances, the task of raising secure and happy adolescents can often seem daunting or even impossible. But God's grace is not held at bay by statistics or hormones.

The good news is that the middle school experience does not need to lead to teenage and young adult years of confusion and heartache. On the contrary, your son or daughter can become an integrated, loving, healthy person. This real possibility is why we have created this guide for parents, why your child has entered into this program, and why St. John Paul II gave us the Theology of the Body (TOB). This message holds a life-changing answer for you and your children, a message that will help them grow into their "real" selves!

The Theology of the Body: A Powerful Message—for Now!

Given the culture in which we live, we need a message of hope that is more powerful than the glitter of society's offerings. This is what the Theology of the Body provides, for it resonates with the deepest desires of the human heart.

That message is none other than the Gospel of Jesus and his Church, a message that transcends time, space, and culture. You may believe that your child has already heard this message. What differs here, though, is the particular emphasis of the Theology of the Body. It is a relevant message, and your son or daughter will find it an exciting one, too.

Collectively, the authors of *Theology of the Body for Teens: Middle School Edition* have given talks to hundreds of thousands of teenagers over the past decade. In our experience, young people *love* this message. They eat up it; they learn to live it.

As parents, you are the primary educators of your children. We want to help you to form them in these critical middle school years. This Parent's Guide offers some concrete ways of reaching your children and loving them as they need to be loved. In keeping with the guidelines set forth by the Pontifical Council for the Family in its document *The Truth and Meaning of Human Sexuality,* this guide also highlights the content that the program will present to your children.[5] You have the "duty and right to be the first and principal educators" of your children;[6] this program aims to supplement and foster the formation you are called to give them.[7]

As Pope Benedict XVI has said, "Of ourselves, we cannot come to terms with ourselves. Our 'I' becomes acceptable only when it has been accepted by another 'I' and is perceived as accepted."[8] What does this mean for you as a parent? Your role is crucial: you are the one who can best lead your son or daughter to discover who he or she really is in Jesus! We pray that the following pages will give you tools to help reveal your child to himself or herself. May you be guided by the Holy Spirit, the giver of life and hope.

Parents Benefit by "Forming Their Children in Love"

Many Catholics have not even heard of the Theology of the Body. Therefore, this Parent's Guide will not only highlight the concepts your child will learn in this program, but will also share several concepts that we hope will deepen your understanding of your own life and vocation, as the Church desires.[9]

Theology of the Body in a Nutshell

The Theology of the Body can be encompassed in one word: *union.* Each of us is destined for union: with God and his creation; within ourselves; and with others.

- **Union With God and With His Creation**
  How do we know that we are made for union? Because God has stamped this truth on our very bodies! Take, for instance, our five senses, which enable us to see, smell, taste, hear, and feel. They are the means by which we receive stimulus from outside of ourselves. Our senses unite us with the goodness of God's creation. Even in the design of our senses, our body "speaks" of openness and receptivity—a language of union. So to be human is first *to receive*, especially to receive God's love and life, thereby entering into union with him.

- **Union Within Ourselves**
  Union within ourselves flows from a pure heart, which then is manifested in the actions of our bodies. In other words, we are called to live integrated lives. John Paul II refers to this integration as *holiness*, which involves speaking the truth with our bodies at all times.

- **Union With Others**
  Union with others is an essential aspect of the Theology of the Body. Human communication and connection occurs

primarily through bodily action, through the "language" of the body. For example, we shake hands, we hug one another, we kiss those we love. In other words, our body shows us that we are meant to be gifts to others, that we are made to love others.

Moreover, union with others is shown in our masculinity and femininity. God made the male and female bodies to be complementary—that is, to go together. The language of the male body and the language of the female body show us that God wants us to be attracted to the opposite sex, to date, to fall in love, to get engaged, and ultimately to marry and form a family. Such a union—the communion of life and love in the family—is meant to reflect God's inner life and love in the Trinity. Not only that, it reflects Jesus' fruitful love for his bride, the Church.

The Theology of the Body: Getting the Whole Picture

St. John Paul II, reflecting on Genesis 1–3 and Ephesians 5, says that marriage is the best natural sign of who God is and that marriage should reflect and participate in the covenant of life and love between Christ and the Church. True union within marriage speaks of God's union with us through Christ. It also speaks of the *ultimate union*: each person of the Blessed Trinity—the Father, Son, and Holy Spirit—is a gift to the other. This eternal exchange of life and love is what we are called to participate in for eternity, starting *now*. Yes, union is the essence of the entire picture God has been painting all along.

Union vs. Rupture

Between 1979 and 1984, John Paul II presented his Theology of the Body as a series of talks that emphasized the human design for union. Union—true love that is given and received—will bring happiness. Division and brokenness lead to sorrow and broken hearts. Such rupture is usually based on the opposite of love. According to John Paul II, the opposite of love is not *hating* others; the opposite of love is *using* others—grasping, taking, and manipulating rather than giving, receiving, and loving. Using others leads to isolation; love leads to union.

Deep down, we all sense that union is the essence of happiness. We can see this trace of understanding in the cultural emphasis on the body and sex. In our current culture, though, the body is often seen as valuable only for what it produces or its degree of physical perfection. Sexual activity is merely for pleasure, like a hobby, empty of meaning. Yet the bitter aftertaste that so many experience in the wake of their failed searches for incarnate love begs us to consider God's plan for our bodies and our sexuality.

The good news is that we, as Christians, are called to be "in the world but not of the world." We are not here to isolate ourselves from society, seeing it as inherently evil; nor are we to accept uncritically the distorted ideas of the world. As St. John Paul II teaches, Jesus "calls to the human heart" to live the truth of the body. So let's get to it!

A Parent's Prayer for Your Child

The following prayer is provided at the end of each chapter. We suggest that you pray it daily. (The wording can be adapted, as needed, for single parents or for additional children.) In addition, a separate prayer based on the specific content of each chapter immediately follows this prayer.

> *Dear God, Father, Son, and Holy Spirit,*
> *You have given us [name of your child], and we are called to love and care for him/her with our whole body and soul. Help us to show [name of your child] who he/she truly is in you! May the Theology of the Body guide us faithfully as a family. Amen.*

How to Form Your Child

Just as Christ showed us his love through words and deeds, parents are called to show love for their children through their words and deeds. Words without action are empty; actions without words are ambiguous.

Conversation (Words)

Every successful coach would agree that the best defense is a strong offense. The same can be said for discussing topics surrounding body image, sexuality, relationships, and chastity. One of the best things you can do as a parent is to initiate the conversation, for this puts you on "offense" rather than "defense." If you do not invite the discussion about these issues, your child will inevitably learn about them from some other, perhaps misguided, source—such as from the media and/or their friends.

As you begin to talk to your son or daughter about these issues, here are some helpful strategies:

- **Ongoing Dialogue vs. "The Talk"** – Don't just have "the talk" with your son or daughter; rather, have an ongoing conversation. Taking the initiative in chatting with them will let them know that you are not afraid of speaking about sensitive topics like sexuality.

- **Special vs. "Scary"** – Speak about sexuality as a special gift from God, rather than as a "scary" topic. Such an approach avoids instilling anxiety in your son or daughter. They will learn to see sex as a wonderful gift that God lovingly bestows on each of us, as an *amazing* gift to be embraced rather than feared.

- **Frank and Reverent vs. Ambiguous and Shameful** – Parents of young children often use euphemisms or "code words" to emphasize that certain parts of the body are to be especially reverenced. But such an approach might give your son or daughter the impression that there is something shameful or "dirty" about sexuality. On the other hand, using slang or "street" words is not a good idea either (except for clarification). Use the correct terms for things in a reverent way.

- **Gift to Be Embraced vs. Evil to Be Repressed** – Expressing to your child that sexuality/chastity is an adventure to embrace underscores the truth that growing up is good. Rather than an evil that needs to be repressed, tell your son or daughter that their sexual desires are a reminder that they are meant to give themselves away totally as a gift, either in marriage or in the priesthood or consecrated life.

- **Truly Present vs. Fragmented Discussions** – Time and attention are what your child needs. When you turn off the technology, stop what you are doing, and sit with your child, you convey the message that you are truly present to your son or daughter. This builds trust so that he or she will want to talk with you about important matters.

- **Context of Marriage vs. Abstract Idea** – Society promotes sex as a fun activity with no restraints or rules as long as

a young person is "ready" and "safe." But John Paul II
reminds us that love goes hand-in-hand with responsibility,
meaning that sexual activity ought to take place within the
secure context of a loving marriage.

- **Context of a Community vs. Individualism** – The idea of the
"common good" is something that our modern culture needs
to reclaim. Too often, discussions concerning sexuality are
focused on the individual. A proper understanding that
sexual decisions affect the common good of the community
is an important observation to emphasize. A pregnant
teenager is not the only one who must deal with the
consequences of her pregnancy; her parents, grandparents,
siblings, unborn child, and, indeed, society as a whole are
affected. No decision is made in a vacuum.

- **Theology *and* Biology**—To limit the conversation about
sexuality to God's moral law without a discussion of its
biology can imply to your child that God expects us to live
by some arbitrary and unrealistic standard. On the other
hand, science by itself cannot speak to the sacredness
of sexuality. While we do not address biological issues
regarding sexuality, your middle schoolers need you to
address these with them. Tell them that their physiological
reactions are not "dirty" or "bad." Such desires remind us
that, in God's design for our bodies, we are called to love, to
union. Later, a discussion on what to do with those desires
will be in order.

Events (Actions)

"Actions speak louder than words" is especially true when trying to
form your child in the area of sexuality. Chastity is the proper ordering
of sexuality within one's particular state of life; all people, married and

non-married alike, are called to practice chastity in the way fitting their vocation. Chastity is more about saying "yes" to love and the responsibility that comes with it than it is about saying "no" to sex. It's about a holistic and generous approach to living our sexuality in the freedom that God desires for us, as framed by the teachings of the Church. Chastity is about self-control and self-sacrifice. This is why chastity *inside* of marriage is such a powerful witness. When you model chastity in your marriage, your child notices.

Here are some ways to reinforce the message of your ongoing conversations:

- **Proper Affection vs. Fear of the Body – Between Parents *and* Between Parents and Children**
    - When you, as parents, embrace and kiss each other in front of your children, you demonstrate to them that your affection runs throughout the course of your day-to-day interaction, and this gives them a sense of security.
    - Whether your child seems to want it or not, he or she still needs a great deal of affection from both parents. Healthy affection teaches your child that his or her body is good and that the appropriate degree of affection depends upon the relationship. Our society has "sexualized" touch, but appropriate parental touch shows your child that not all touch is sexual, that it can speak the language of familial love.

- **Special Dates and Intentional Interaction**
    - *With Each Other:* One way to give security to your child is to go on regular "dates" with each other, sharing one-on-one time in an intentional way. Good trainers know developing a particular muscle group in your body requires core strengthening exercises first. Similarly, the conscious upkeep of your marital relationship stabilizes

children by showing that you love each other and that you are committed to your marriage vows—and to them. Your marriage is the core of your family; strengthening your love for one another will make your children feel secure.

- *With Your Child:* The most well-adjusted children are those whose parents give them frequent one-on-one time. This shows them that they are an important focus of your life, despite your busy schedule. Your presence is worth more than presents! Such time should not replace, but complement, your everyday interactions.

- **Leading by Example vs. By Words Only** – Teens have a nearly infallible "authenticity detector." They are experts at detecting insincerity and hypocrisy. "Do as I say, not as I do" devalues any open dialogue you may have established. If the Church teaches one thing but you do the opposite, your child sees and is formed by this example. In contrast, parents who are active in the life of the Church by participating in the sacraments (especially the Eucharist and reconciliation) and serving the poor are the ones who raise children who take their Catholic faith—and their sexuality—seriously.

- **Loving Guidance vs. "Hands Off" Attitude** – When your child says, "Mom, you're way too overbearing" or "Dad, can't you just leave me alone?" don't take their words too seriously. You might remember saying something similar to your own parents as a teenager. Your teens want and need structure and guidance in the area of sexuality and in other areas, too.

Here are some examples:

- A reasonable curfew. Too strict a curfew shows you don't trust your middle schooler. Too lax a curfew can convey the idea that you don't really care.

- Go shopping with your daughter— especially dads. Not only will you have to say, "No" (*Too low cut! Not long enough! No words on your backside!*), but you will also get a chance to say, "Yes!" (*That looks great! It's flattering! That color brings out your eyes!*) In other words, you will have a place to articulate the reasons for your decisions. This kind of interaction is excellent formation regarding modest attire. It is also essential for adolescents to receive abundant amounts of praise and affirmation from their family. Make sure to praise them at least twice as often as you criticize.

- It is imperative for fathers to show their sons attention. Teaching a son tricks of a trade, financial planning, how to camp, how to play sports—all of these teach a young man what it means to be a man: sacrifice and embodied love.

One

Who Am I?

Discovering My True Identity

Remember when Mapquest first came on the scene? How could it map out our route and give us directions so quickly—for *free?!* Of course, for all of its dazzle, Mapquest would be useless without having a starting point and a destination. Only when the user plugs in the correct information can the magic happen.

In Chapter 1 of the *Middle School Edition*, we introduce a similar "map analogy" to your child: Your child will not be free to be himself or herself until he or she understands our *origin* and our *destiny*. The map we explore in this chapter gets to the heart of our beginnings and our final goal. Your child will do the following:

- Ask some fundamental questions about his or her identity and what it means to be human.

- Explore the basic nature of growing up.

- Learn what true freedom is and its purpose.

- Understand how Jesus' Incarnation reveals the truth about his or her life.

- Discover the Theology of the Body as God's "map," given to help us find our way to true fulfillment as human persons.

Finding Myself Before God

In the presentations of the Theology of the Body, John Paul II speaks of how Adam was "alone before God in search of his identity." Seeing ourselves as God sees us unveils who we really are, showing us that our ultimate identity lies in our relationship with God.

At this crucial time in your child's life, he or she often looks to peers for affirmation and approval, to receive his or her identity. In this chapter, we discuss this tendency and encourage your child to think beyond surface values, such as popularity, looks, or extra-curricular activities. Instead, we invite them deeper, toward

"If you are what you should be, you will set the world on fire."

– St. Catherine of Siena

something that reveals our true human identity.

Scripture says, "Deep calls to deep" (Psalm 42:7). God, the deepest mystery, calls us to the very depths of who we are. What is the "ultimate depth" of God? He is love (see 1 John 4:7-8). And what is our depth? That we have been made for love. Each person is intimately, uniquely designed by God, made in his image and likeness. We were conceived in love by God and by our parents—our origin. We are made for love and heaven—our goal. With this starting point and destination, the map of the Theology of the Body guides us, while helping us to see meaning in our choices here and now.

As your child matures, the choices he or she makes bear more impact and demand more responsibility. Part of your task is to provide *security* to help growth in *maturity* on the road to *purity.* Guiding children to embrace their true identity enables them to make proper choices, both short and long term.

St. John Paul II speaks about Adam experiencing "original solitude." We adapt this concept for early adolescents: each person determines his or her own life. Each of us is entirely unlike anyone else. In fact, the uniqueness of your child's body underscores the uniqueness of his or her person. Your child's soul, which is invisible, is revealed by the visible, the body.

Another of your tasks is to affirm the individuality of your child and to assist him or her toward discovering his or her identity. We sometimes try to make God in our own image and likeness; parents sometimes try to make their children in their own image and likeness. *Forming* is very different from *forcing*.

The Gift of Freedom: To Love

Whereas middle school students often see freedom as license and independence from authority, this program challenges them to see the truth—that freedom's ultimate purpose is to enable us to truly love.

This is the essence of being human: loving. Robots can't love. A sunset can't love you. Remember that the goal of the Theology of the Body is union, and without love, union cannot be achieved. You can help your children to understand this challenging truth.

> *"Man ... cannot fully find himself except through a sincere gift of himself."*
> – Gaudium et Spes 24

Remember to pray for your child.

Prayer for Your Child

Dear God, Father, Son, and Holy Spirit,
You have given us [name of your child], *and we are called to love and care for him/her with our whole body and soul. Help us to show* [name of your child] *who he/she truly is in you!*
May the Theology of the Body guide us faithfully as a family.
Amen.

"Who Am I?" Prayer for Your Child

Lord, our child needs our help in becoming his/her true self. Give us the wisdom to know how to direct him/her according to your divine plan and for his/her good. Amen.

Questions for Your Middle Schooler:

1. Who are the most popular kids in your class? Why are they popular? What do you think is a good reason to be popular? Do you wish you were more popular? Why or why not?
2. Who is the funniest person in your class? A good sense of humor is a gift. What gifts do you think you offer to your class? (Help your child see his or her gifts, using concrete examples of when you've seen those gifts in action).
3. If you could choose what you want to be when you grow up—anything at all—what would it be? Why?
4. I remember when I was your age trying to figure out who I was. It was often confusing. What is most confusing for you? What is the hardest thing to deal with?

FAMILY APPLICATIONS

1. **Mission Statements:** Create mission statements, listing goals and ways to achieve them.

    a. Write a family mission statement.

    b. Help your middle schooler write his or her own mission statement.

    Writing a mission statement reinforces the map analogy, helping your child know who he or she is and where he or she is going. The goals and objectives (concrete daily choices) then become attached to a bigger goal in life.

2. **Family Tree:** Make a family tree and list the main gifts and talents of each person in your (immediate or extended) family. Notice the uniqueness of each person.

3. **Photo-Growth:** Scan photographs of your child, from an *in utero* sonogram to the present. Put them in a photo album or in a multi-picture frame. Write a note on the back telling your child how you have watched him or her grow. Elaborate on the difficulties of middle school years, but how you plan to support him or her through it all.

RECOMMENDATIONS FOR FURTHER STUDY

For your child:

- *The Book of Virtues* by William Bennett
- *The Hobbit* by J.R.R. Tolkien

For your own personal growth:

- *Healing the Unaffirmed* by Conrad Baars
- *TOB and Healing Workshops* by Dr. Bob Schuchts (available at tobhealing.org)
- *Redemptor Hominis (The Redeemer of Man)*, encyclical letter of St. John Paul II
- *I Believe in Love: A Personal Retreat based on the Teaching of St. Thérèse of Lisieux* by Fr. Jean C.J. d'Elbee
- *Strong Fathers, Strong Daughters* by Meg Meeker

Two

Our Story

God's Plan, Human Sin, Jesus' Love

The following is a true story. One day, I noticed that there was a small, inch-high pile of what looked like sawdust in my bedroom. "Hmmm," I thought, but not knowing what to make of it, I did nothing. A week later, the formerly inch-high pile was now three inches high. I again thought, "Uh-oh. Something's wrong. But I am too busy to worry about it, so I'll just ignore it." Another week went by—and a much higher pile of sawdust appeared. "Okay. I have to face it. I must find out what is going on." So I called a couple of friends, and one suggested that I call an exterminator, fearing that termites might be the culprit. The exterminator came and issued his verdict: carpenter ants!

He had to drill eighteen holes in my bedroom wall and spray poison in the holes to reach the ants inside. If I hadn't finally addressed the issue and turned to experts for help, part of my house could have fallen down.

~Monica Ashour

God's plan for our lives does not include sin and destruction. We are always meant to be safe and secure under his protection. Yet sin enters in, just like the ants in our story entered into a place so dark and hidden that their presence was not immediately obvious. We don't like to look at those issues in our lives, the "sawdust clues" that point out that something is amiss.

> *"So God created man in his own image, in the image of God he created him; male and female he created them." – Genesis 1:27*

Yet God's love can penetrate those places of our hearts where we have allowed sin to exist. Jesus can eradicate our faults and sins. Sometimes, we may need the help of a counselor or spiritual director to help us heal our respective wounds, faults, or sins. Healing often hurts. But Jesus, the true carpenter, can forgive us and rebuild us ... if we acknowledge our need and allow his healing touch to purify our hearts.

This chapter recalls the Christian story of our beginning, fall, redemption, and resurrection—and how each person participates in this story. In his Theology of the Body, John Paul II describes these movements as "Original Man" (where we came from; humanity before the Fall), "Historical Man" (where we are now), and "Eschatological Man" (where we are going). Especially important is for middle schoolers to understand that they have free will—that they can choose to do good or evil. Sin matters because sin hurts union. But Jesus sets us free to love.

In Chapter 2, your child will do the following:

- Explore God's original plan for humanity.

- Understand original sin as a lost inheritance.

- Reflect on the experience of sin as a counterfeit of good.

- Anticipate the hope and healing Jesus brings.

Concupiscence and Con Artists

The tendency to sin, known as *concupiscence*, is due to the Fall, the original sin of our first parents. Before the Fall, our desires were perfectly ordered toward the good; now, however, we often desire that which is not good for us. "Eve saw that the tree was good for food" despite the fact that God had explicitly said not to eat from it (see Genesis 3:6). St. John Paul II says that Adam and Eve fell because they "doubted the gift." In other words, they began to see God as a tyrant who wanted to bring them down, rather than as a loving father who wanted to give them "every good gift" (see James 1:17).

As parents, you are the first representatives of God to your children as well as their first example of his loving law. Thus, consider that as you show your total, unconditional love for your child, you can show you are not a tyrant. Instead, parents should give appropriate rules (neither overbearing nor lax) and consistently enforce them. Of course, a typical middle schooler may often *perceive* you as a tyrant, but remember that God, who banished his children from the Garden of Eden, sent his only Son to heal us and his Holy Spirit to give us hope and strength.

The most powerful con artist in the world is the devil. In fact, he is known as the "great deceiver," who is *diabolos* ("slanderer" or "accuser"). He cons us into thinking sin is good, and when we fall for it, we experience division. This chapter presents several examples of division to your child:

- Between the body and the soul (i.e., death).

- Between us and nature (e.g. pain, defects, disease).

- Between us and others (hurt, backstabbing, divorce, the end of a relationship).

- Between us and God (a smaller spiritual death—*venial sin*— or a grave spiritual death—*mortal sin*).

How are we so deceived? The devil rarely tempts us with something that is obviously and repulsively evil. Were that the case, we wouldn't be attracted to it, and thus would not choose it. Instead, we are conned by counterfeits, fabricated fakes, and impious imposters.

> *When we renew our Baptismal promises, we say, "I do" to the question, "Do you reject the glamour of evil and refuse to be mastered by sin?"* – RCIA Study Edition, 219

Chapter two compares temptation to email spam. The glitter and glamour of pop-ups promises pleasure. But when pursued, spam infects our computer and slows down its processing speed. Then the spam perpetuates; if not corrected, it can overwhelm the entire hard drive.

It is important to train your child's truth, beauty, and goodness detector. Point out scams and distortions in the media. Underscore that these counterfeits appeal to good desires, but that they are twisted. Remind them that Our Lady was sinless because she never fell for the counterfeit; she only loved. Her union with God was so deep that she gave the greatest life to the world: her son, Jesus, who heals us. From union to rupture to healing to eternal union: for this we were made.

Remember to pray for your child.

Prayer for Your Child

Dear God, Father, Son, and Holy Spirit,
You have given us [name of your child], *and we are called to love and care for him/her with our whole body and soul. Help us to show* [name of your child] *who he/she truly is in you! May the Theology of the Body guide us faithfully as a family. Amen.*

"Our Story" Prayer for Your Child

Mother Mary, you who refused to be mastered by the glamour of evil, pray for our family. Ask your son to give us strength to recognize evil and reject it. Jesus, help me face the sawdust of my life and heal me so I might better guide my child. Amen.

Questions for Your Middle Schooler:

1. Why do you think some kids in your class misbehave? What are they looking for? What do they think they will get by disobeying?
2. What do you think are the main temptations for people your age? What is the counterfeit that is tricking some of your friends?
3. When I was your age, I remember thinking that my parents were dumb, didn't understand me, and didn't want me to have any fun. Maybe I seem that way to you sometimes. But do you know that all I really want is what is best for you? Can we talk about some times lately when you thought I was unreasonable?
4. Remember that you learned that sin brings division. Do you feel the divisions created by sin? What is it like? Who is affected?

FAMILY APPLICATIONS

1. **Spiritual "I Spy":** Invite your child to join you in keeping a log of all of the glamorized, superficial temptations you and your child see every day. This is like a spiritual "I Spy" game. After a week, come back together to show each other what you found and how the temptations are counterfeits to good. You might have a contest for who can come up with the most.

2. **Family Examination and Confession:** Explain to your child that in every sacrament, we meet Christ, who heals division. Before heading to confession, give your child an examination of conscience and tell him or her to bring a journal to write in. Explain that this journal is private, between your child and God, and that you will not read it. While in line for confession, model your own examination of conscience by writing in your own journal. Afterward, pray and journal in front of the Blessed Sacrament. When driving home, ask about what struck him or her most about the experience of forgiveness.

RECOMMENDATIONS FOR FURTHER STUDY

For your child:

- *The Lion, the Witch, and the Wardrobe* by C.S. Lewis

For your own personal growth:

- *The Evidential Power of Beauty* by Fr. Thomas Dubay (Addresses how to foster a proper appreciation for real beauty)
- *Freedom: Twelve Lives Transformed by the Theology of the Body*, edited by Matthew Pinto
- *The Great Divorce* by C.S. Lewis
- *Raising Pure Teens* by Jason Evert and Chris Stefanick

Chapter Three

Me, Myself, and I
Body and Soul

The smile. Several years ago, you smiled at your newborn baby for the first time. That was the first spiritual act of the universe for your child.[10] How so? The visible reveals the invisible. Through the "language of your body," you revealed your deep love for your child, and you elicited a response. Soon, your baby learned to smile back. Union happened.

Parents are the first representatives of God to their children. God is constantly saying, "I love you" and eliciting a response from each of us. Your smile and the response of your child—physical manifestations of a spiritual act—mirror the love of God and thus bond you more closely.

You continue to reveal your love for your child through the "language of your body." You take him to soccer practice. You read her a book.

> *Jesus shows us what it means to be truly human and makes our calling clear! (See CCC 1701, GS 22.)*

You make his favorite meal. You spend quality time with her. These bodily actions reveal your love for your child and give him a sense of security—even if he or she does not seem to appreciate everything that you do. Keep it up!

In this chapter we introduce the term the "language of the body" to your child and seek to help them do the following:

- Understand that the "language of the body" means to make invisible things visible.

- Understand and reflect on the human person as a body–soul composite.

- Confront and discuss spiritual and emotional issues related to the body.

- Reflect on the Son of God becoming human while remaining divine and how the "language of his body" speaks to us about what it means to be human.

The "Language of the Body" as a Guide

In Germany, the traditional wedding vows are "I am yours; you are mine." These words, and others like them (e.g., "until death do us part"), express the permanent and indissoluble nature of marriage. These same words "become flesh" when the marriage is consummated, and they are renewed throughout a couple's life. When St. John Paul II coined the term "language of the body," his explicit meaning was that of conjugal love.

In teaching your child, we begin by discussing many gestures of the body that show how the body speaks a language. Why is this so revolutionary and life-changing? Because the "language of the body" takes the simple concepts of "body language" to a whole new level!

We know a person's inner emotions through facial expressions, gestures, and other actions. But the language of the body goes even further. This truth proclaims that the body makes the invisible *soul* of a person visible through what is conveyed through one's body. St. John Paul II says it like this: "The body, in fact, and only the body, is capable of making visible what is invisible: the spiritual and divine. It has been created to transfer into the visible reality of the world the mystery hidden from eternity in God, and thus to be a sign of it" (TOB 19:4).

The soul and the body must coincide, or "match," for a person to have integrity. This is why the actions of the body must speak the truth of God's love. God's invisible love, in our invisible souls, is made visible by the loving actions we do in and through the body.

To a modern culture steeped in the relativistic idea that each person can subjectively decide what is right or wrong, John Paul II underscored an objective truth that no one can deny and all should obey: the body must "speak" a universal language of truth and love.

Imagine the following demonstration of this universal truth: A volunteer is given a doll and told to express his love for this "little sister" by tickling her cheek and saying, "Coochy-coo." Of course, it's funny. Then, the volunteer is instructed to express his love by yelling right in the doll's face. This time, it's even funnier! But why do we laugh? Because something is amiss! To show love by such a gesture just doesn't fit. It would be like meeting someone, saying, "Nice to meet you," and then slugging him. The bodily action does not fit the internal disposition. Those expressions, then, are lies.

John Paul II tells us that we are to "re-read the 'language of the body' in truth." Objective truth exists. And we can know and experience this truth through the body, for it speaks a universal language that transcends time and culture. True, one culture may bow or another may greet with a kiss when meeting, but no culture greets another with a punch!

This essential concept lays the foundation for your child regarding the rightness or wrongness of various actions, not just in the arena of sexuality, but in the totality of his or her life. More on this later. This chapter establishes that to be truly human is for body and soul to be a composite.

The Word (Spiritual) Made Flesh (Physical)

When God became man, the Word was made flesh; the God who is pure spirit took on a physical body. Indeed, God took on a fully human nature. Here is something that may surprise your middle schooler: Jesus did not skip puberty! He experienced adolescence within the context of his culture just as your middle schooler experiences adolescence within the context of our culture. Yet because he was like us in all things but sin (see Hebrews 4:15), Jesus responded with perfectly ordered love in every situation. Your child's struggles and temptations *can* be overcome through Jesus' grace, which we receive in a special way when we meet him in the sacraments.

> *"The body, and the body alone, makes visible the invisible: the spiritual and the divine."*
> *– St. John Paul II*

The Theology of the Body gives us words to guide us to the truth of love, the truth of being human, the truth of being happy. He first points us to the One, Jesus Christ, the Incarnate son who shows us what it means to be fully human.[11] St. Irenaeus said, "The Son of God became human so that humans can become sons [and daughters] of God." This is the essence of Christianity, which means it is the essence of life: union with Christ and his bride the Church.

This is good news.

Remember to pray for your child.

Prayer for Your Child

> *Dear God, Father, Son, and Holy Spirit,*
> *You have given us* [name of your child], *and we are called to love and care for him/her with our whole body and soul. Help us to show* [name of your child] *who he/she truly is in you!*
> *May the Theology of the Body guide us faithfully as a family.*
> *Amen.*

"Body and Soul" Prayer for Your Child

*Jesus, you who reveal to us fully what it means to be human,
help our child to always live an authentic and loving life,
with body and soul together. Give us, too, the wisdom to live
according to the "language of the body." Amen.*

Questions for Your Middle Schooler:

1. What does your teacher do that tells you he or she is
    angry? What is the language of his or her body? What
    about when he or she is happy? What do I do when I am
    mad?
2. When did I not pay attention to the language of *your*
    body when I should have? What can I do to be more
    sensitive to you?
3. I know sometimes kids are mean, make fun of each
    other, and point out what appear to be flaws in someone
    else's body. Who gets picked on in your class? Why? Are
    you ever made fun of? How does it make you feel?
4. When you think of Jesus, do you think of Him as only
    God? What are some things that Jesus—who was totally
    human with a body—went through that you may never
    have considered before?

FAMILY APPLICATION:

1. **Family Night:** Announce an upcoming family night. (Pick a night when no extracurricular activities are scheduled.) Make a special dinner or order out. Turn off all technology. Gather in the living room and play charades. Every now and then, mention the term "the language of the body" to reinforce how what they learn can be applied in life.

2. **Heart-to-Heart:** Have a "heart-to-heart" night. During the "heart-to-heart," come up with one question or topic and have your child do the same. You can do this two ways: through a weekly conversation or a weekly journal. Boys may appreciate a five- to ten-minute chat more than the journal option. If you choose the journal, write down the questions in the "heart-to-heart" journal you bought or made, and write for five minutes about one of the topics. (You may also consider letting your child help "name" the journal, if "heart-to-heart" doesn't seem to fit.) Then, take five minutes to write about the topic. Exchange journals, and read what the other person wrote. The idea here is not to have a marathon interaction. It can be deliberately kept short, so as not to be overbearing for you or your child. Whether conversation or journal, respond to what the other says. End with a hug of affirmation and love.

   • **Suggested Topic:** A suggested topic is maturation. Tell your daughter about how girls go through puberty and how their monthly cycle affects them emotionally—sometimes they cry without knowing why, sometimes they are grouchy, sometimes they want to be alone. Tell your son about how boys go through puberty—their voice changes, they get taller, they begin to have strong feelings for girls—and they sometimes don't know what to do with such changes. Then, ask your son or daughter about what he or she is feeling—about others and about growing up and experiencing these changes. These are a few ways that the invisible nature of male and female adolescent growth is made visible through bodily maturation.

• **Note the Distinctions:** Consider some of the differences between boys and girls. Boys often bond through activities, whereas girls bond more through conversation. Boys might listen better when they're not sitting still. This is the reason why men often pace while on the phone. With your daughter, grabbing a smoothie or an ice cream or just taking a walk can set a nice space for conversation. With your son, consider tossing a ball in the backyard or maybe taking him fishing, or for a drive. While doing active things, talk about what matters.

RECOMMENDATIONS FOR FURTHER STUDY

For your child:

• *All Things Girl* (series) by Teresa Tomeo, Molly Miller, and Monica Cops

• *The Lord of the Rings* by J.R.R. Tolkien

For your own personal growth:

• *Theology of the Body for Beginners* by Christopher West

• *Chance or the Dance* by Thomas Howard

Chapter Four

How Should I Act?

When an unusually intense ice storm occurs, it is not uncommon to see lots of big branches on the ground and even a huge tree or two toppled over. Some trees cannot withstand the weight of the ice and snow, so they collapse. When the exterior pressure is too great, the tree topples over.

Human beings are a bit like these trees. Without the self-mastery spoken of in the Theology of the Body, we will be unable to withstand temptations from outside influences and we might "fall over" into sin. With the life of the Holy Spirit, we can be people of integrity. Just as a bridge is measured by its "integrity"—i.e., by how much pressure it can withstand—so too the life of a human is measured by one's integrity, or virtue.

In this chapter, your child will learn about being a person of integrity, which makes us truly human by forming character. Your child will also do the following:

- Differentiate between virtue and vice, their nature and effects.

- Explore their own habits, especially in the area of social networking, cell phones, and computers.

- Understand the need for consistency in the practice of virtue vs. multiple "selves."

- Explore and participate in the sacramental life of the Church.

Practice Makes Perfect

Given the immediacy of contemporary life—of getting things when we want them, how we want them, in the way we want them—it is difficult for us to adopt the gradual process of growing in virtue. The analogy here is of practicing drills and exercises, day-after-day, to become proficient on a musical instrument. Such skill is impossible without dedicated practice on a daily basis.

Your son or daughter needs you as a coach to help form him or her into a virtuous person. In this crucial time, your son or daughter needs rules, structure, reinforcement, and consistency, so that later, your guidance will not be necessary, because the virtuous life has become second nature.

Consider a "tree analogy": Often, after an enormous tree branch falls onto a house and causes roof damage, experts are called to remove it and repair the roof. These experts will often insert cables to reinforce the remaining branches to avoid another accident. As a parent, you establish rules that act much like these cables. They are external supports to keep everything from crashing down. Like tree braces, your rules are in place until your child develops strong virtue "branches" to withstand temptations, especially those that flow from peer pressure. Your guidance is crucial at this point in your middle schooler's development.

Forming your child now in virtues such as patience, honesty, fortitude, and perseverance will have lasting ramifications. It will give them the tools to pursue eternal life with God in heaven. How do you do this? By showing your children what virtue is and what is expected of them. Therefore, they will know in their

> *"The virtuous person tends toward the good with all his sensory and spiritual powers; he pursues the good and chooses it in concrete actions. The goal of the virtuous life is to become like God." – CCC 1803*

hearts what they should do, and they will make the language of their bodies correspond. When you see that the virtues have become second nature to them, you can then give them more freedom and responsibility. This will allow them to practice on more significant things until those things, too, become second nature. Adulthood will follow. Moreover, giving more freedom and responsibility at the right time shows trust in your child, which fosters a strong, lifelong relationship with him or her.

Piety and the "REs" of Marital Intercourse

While we don't speak to your middle schooler about this,[12] you may be surprised at which virtue St. John Paul II says is the most needed regarding conjugal love: piety. Piety! Isn't piety acting pious, i.e., praying and performing religious devotions? Partly. The Latin root for "piety" is *pietas*, which has to do with having reverence for one's homeland, ancestors, and especially God.[13] In the case of marital love, Pope John Paul II underscores the piety owed to one's spouse and to God who created the body with its particular language. When couples take a pious approach to each other, they

- REspect ("look again" at) each other,

- REmind ("call to mind again") themselves to...

- REmember ("call to memory again") with...

- REverence ("to venerate again") the vows they made to each other before God and others on their wedding day.

The virtue of piety solidifies and strengthens love.

"Blessed are the pure in heart, for they shall see God." – Matthew 5:8

As you teach piety to your child in its various forms, you are forming him or her for a future vocation to marriage, priesthood, or consecrated life. Such formation starts now. Sometimes, family members don't remember to see each other properly. Take a step back and *remember* with *reverence* your child … his or her amazing birth, first toddling steps, first words, and endearing traits.

Remember to pray for your child.

Prayer for Your Child

Dear God, Father, Son, and Holy Spirit,
You have given us [name of your child], *and we are called to love and care for him/her with our whole body and soul. Help us to show* [name of your child] *who he/she truly is in you!*
May the Theology of the Body guide us faithfully as a family.
Amen.

"How Should I Act" Prayer for Your Child

Dear Holy Spirit, give [name of your child] *Your loving power so that he/she grows in virtue, becoming a true man/woman of God. Amen.*

Questions for Your Middle Schooler:

1. When you are sharing something important with a friend, and you are interrupted because he or she receives a text or call, how do you feel? Why do you think you feel that way?
2. What are some of the main vices that your friends and classmates struggle with? Why do you suppose that is?
3. I noticed that you have grown in the virtue of *[name the virtue]* as of late. (Mention a concrete moment when you saw the virtue in action.) I am very proud of you. How does it feel to live with that virtue as a real part of your life?
4. I remember when I was your age that I sometimes acted differently around certain people to be considered cool. I later realized I should just be myself. Around what people do you find it hard to be yourself? Why?

FAMILY APPLICATION:

1. **The Three-Day Mission**: Jonah was in the whale's belly for three days. Jesus was in the tomb three days. Your family "mission" for three days will be this: No texting, phone calls, TV, or Internet (the only exception is for school assignments or work.). The goal here is to experience three days of silence to get in touch with the mystery of yourself and your family members. Aristotle said that to develop virtue, one must go to the opposite extreme to get to the mean. Discuss how to use technology in a virtuous way. If three entire days seems too long, set aside a few hours each day (e.g. 4:00 to 8:00 p.m.).

2. **Virtue Project:** Join your child in doing the Virtue Bead program suggested in his or her workbook. Let your child explain to you the process so that he or she takes more ownership.

3. **Antidote for Venom**: Read together one chapter of Peter Kreeft's *Snakebite Letters* per night and discuss how the devil does not want us living a virtuous life and how the Catholic ER (the sacraments of the Eucharist and reconciliation) can help.

RECOMMENDATIONS FOR FURTHER STUDY

For your child:

- *Snakebite Letters* by Peter Kreeft

- *Do I Have to Go? 101 Questions About the Mass, the Eucharist, and Your Spiritual Life* by Matthew Pinto and Chris Stefanick

For your own personal growth:

- *Back to Virtue* by Peter Kreeft

- *The Three Philosophies of Life* by Peter Kreeft

- *Self-Mastery Checklist* by Monica Ashour

Chapter Five

Sex, Love, and Chastity

I saw him live. I saw him die. I saw Erin kiss him as he breathed his last.

Zack and Erin had a beautiful wedding and a great marriage, but after a couple of transplants, his cystic fibrosis was getting the better of him. I went to St. Paul's Hospital in Dallas every day to be with Zack in his final days. I remember crying with Erin because we thought that he would not make it to their fifth anniversary. He proved us wrong, and I still believe that, even in his coma, God granted Zack's last desire to be able to leave this earth on June 20th, their fifth anniversary.

> *"We must never forget that only when love between human beings is put to the test can its true value be seen."*
> *– Pope John Paul II*

What if every married couple reflected on their limited amount of days together? Would they be as committed to loving each other as Zack and Erin were? Far from society's view of sex separated from sacrament, Zack and Erin lived their marriage in committed love, through thick and thin.

~Monica Ashour

In the previous four chapters, we set forth a comprehensive, foundational approach to what it means to be human and how to act. Now, we will delve deeply into the issue of sexuality. Your child will now explore the meaning of sex and its relationship to marriage as well as the following:

- Consider why there are two genders, their equality and complementarity.

- Consider how gender identity as a man or woman affects the question, "Who am I?"

- Consider the meaning of sexual identity in light of Adam and Eve's original experience.

- Consider how the principle of selfishness vs. self-gift applies to sexuality.

- Apply the truths about the language of the body and Jesus' standard for truly human behavior to sexuality.

- Determine that chastity is a positive virtue of sexual purity, not merely the practice of abstinence, and that lust is a vice.

- Understand how chastity gives us freedom in our relationships to truly love and fulfill our intended purpose.

Sexual Desire is Holy?

Yes! Because God invented it. Far from the two extreme approaches offered by our culture—repression or indulgence—this program takes middle schoolers on the journey to the proper understanding of sexuality as given to us by God. In his Theology of the Body, St. John Paul II underscores the fact that we are created male and female with sexual desires so that we might eventually enter into a fruitful communion of life and love (a family) that emulates the Blessed Trinity, whom St. John Paul II refers to as the "First Family."

> "God is love, and he who abides in love abides in God, and God in him." – 1 John 4:16

Having established that attraction to the opposite sex is holy because it is God-given, we again emphasize that selfishness and self-gratification are not loving ways of acting. The virtue of chastity must take root, starting in one's pure heart that guides bodily actions and guards against the vice of lust that uses another.

The Language of the Body Revisited

We have applied the "language of the body" to body-soul integrity. Now we zero in on how specific gestures of the body reveal particular relationships. We hug family members and friends, not strangers. We kiss our loved ones, not our teachers. We genuflect to Jesus present in the tabernacle, not to anyone else. And the most intimate expression of the body, sexual intercourse (indeed, all sexual activity), is reserved for marriage. Why? Because the language of the body "speaks" about the sort of relationship that exists.

The language of sexual activity says, "I am committed only to you for life, no matter what, and I am open to being a parent with you." To engage in sexual activity before marriage is a lie; one is lying with the body rather than speaking truth. The language of the body is proclaiming one message, but the reality of the relationship is not so. For your child, then, practicing abstinence is a way of being honest with one's body and of preparing for marital chastity.

Some youth ministers or teachers may decide to bring in more controversial issues and address them to the group. Others may address them only if their middle schoolers bring them up. Consider asking what sensitive topics your child will be taught.

Remember to pray for your child:

Prayer for Your Child

> *Dear God, Father, Son, and Holy Spirit,*
> *You have given us* [name of your child], *and we are called to love and care for him/her with our whole body and soul. Help us to show* [name of your child] *who he/she truly is in you! May the Theology of the Body guide us faithfully as a family. Amen.*

"Sex, Love, and Chastity" Prayer for Your Child

St. John Paul II, you coined the term the "language of the body." Please pray with us to God for [name of your child], *asking that he/she will live according to the language of his/her body. Amen.*

Questions for Your Middle Schooler:

1. What do you think about the term the "language of the body" regarding sex? Does it make sense to you?

2. It is normal for people your age to deal with sexual desires. God invented sexual desire, so it must be good. This does not mean, however, that it is easy to direct it in a good way. What are some ways that you have noticed awkwardness or struggles of you and your peers to direct sexual desires in a good way?

3. Would you like to share about someone you might be attracted to in your class? Why do you think he or she is cute? (Even if your child does not entertain this question, they will begin to understand that discussing attractions and desires is a good thing in your eyes, not something bad or to be avoided.)

4. What do you think was the most important thing you learned from this chapter?

FAMILY APPLICATION:

1. **TV Talk:** Whenever you watch TV together with your child, be intentional about defending the beauty of God's plan for us whenever the body, sex, or marriage is made fun of or denigrated. Even during a family show or a sporting event, there are often commercials that offer you an excellent teaching opportunity. Rather than shifting uncomfortably and rolling your eyes point out to your middle schooler the emptiness of the "bad example" (whatever it may be) and reassure him or her of the great truths of our Catholic faith. When a show is blatantly offensive, there is no more powerful statement than turning it off, discussing your reasons for this, and holding firm to that decision, even if your middle schooler is upset and argues. Deep down, your son or daughter will respect the fact that you stand for something and are willing to discuss it with them, even if he or she doesn't agree at the moment. Lastly, be sure to praise the media when they represent the body, sex, and marriage with proper respect. This will remind your child that you are not out to spoil his or her fun, but to help him or her stay on the right track.

2. **Heart-to-Heart:** Have a "Heart-to-Heart" Night. (Refer to Chapter 2 for an explanation.) Suggested topic this month: *Why does God give sexual desire?* To point us toward our desire for union with him, to unite us in love that brings forth more life, to give us a foretaste of our ultimate union with Him. *What are ways for those who are not married to work through sexual desire in a loving, non-selfish, wholesome way?* Prayer, strong friendships, healthy interests, and activities such as sports and music; frequent reception of the sacraments of the Eucharist and reconciliation.

3. **Story Time:** In story form, and without judgment, share with your son or daughter some of the bad sexual choices that a friend, colleague, or family member went through. Pick a story of someone they would not be tempted to judge. (Depending on your child's maturation and your relationship, you could bring up some of your own "past," less-than-perfect choices, if you feel this would be helpful; this should be done extremely carefully, remembering that your child is still young and may not be able to handle the responsibility of this information.) Explain all the ramifications.

   Sharing the story of someone your son or daughter <u>does not know</u> can be prudent, as opposed to sharing a story about their Uncle Tom or family friend Mrs. Smith. Otherwise, you may be setting up an awkward moment at the next major family function or at the supermarket. Taking care not to scandalize anyone in this process is also a witness from which your child will learn.

   Finally, tell a story of a saint (or some other virtuous person) who sacrificed and resisted temptation—and the happiness he or she experienced later due to their faithfulness.

RECOMMENDATIONS FOR FURTHER STUDY

For your child:

- *Pure Love, Pure Manhood, Pure Womanhood (small booklets)* by Jason and Crystalina Evert

- *If You Loved Me: 100 Questions on Dating, Relationships, and Sexual Purity* by Jason Evert

For your own personal growth:

- *Good News About Sex and Marriage* by Christopher West

- *How to Teach Teens the Theology of the Body* by Monica Ashour

- *How to Talk to Your Teens about Chastity* by Jason Evert

- *Discovering the Feminine Genius* by Katrina Zeno

Chapter Six

To Use or Not to Use?
That Is the Question

The Opposite of Love

The following seven-word statement by St. John Paul II shatters our culture's way of living: "The opposite of love is to use." So, the opposite of love is not hatred, but using others as objects. How often do we use our families, calling them only when we need them? Or our friends, wanting only to get something from them? Perhaps we even use God, only going to him when we *need* something.

> *"Only the chaste man and the chaste woman are capable of true love." – St. John Paul II*

Of course, we should receive help from God and others, but if the only time we interact with them is to *get* something, then we ought to take a hard look at ourselves.

Chapter 6 conveys this simple concept to your child and helps him or her to do the following:

• Differentiate between love and lust.

• Evaluate contemporary culture and specific behaviors with the standards of chastity (e.g. music, TV, Internet use, pornography, "sexting," premarital sex, etc.).

• Apply the mandate of never using another person to dating behavior and sexual relationships.

• Develop concrete actions to *love* people and to *use* things.

God Never Objectifies Us; He Loves Us!

Lust vs. Love
• Lust takes, Love gives
• Lust forces, Love receives
• Lust divides, Love bonds

In the early 1980s, after a TOB talk, the press reported John Paul II's remark that a husband ought not lust after his wife. One commentator retorted, "If we can't lust after our own wives, who can we lust after?" No one! We are not to use another person, especially our husband or wife, as an object. Another way of putting this is that the *only* proper response to every person is love. From the criminal in prison to the baby in the womb, love is "the one thing necessary" (see Luke 10:42).

Pope Benedict XVI saw his pontificate as a continuation of his predecessor's project. No wonder that his first encyclical letter to the Church, *Deus Caritas Est* ("God is Love"), was about love, especially erotic love. Far from condemning *eros*, Pope Benedict made a shocking statement: God has *eros* for us! Although this mature concept is not shared in the Student Workbook, your child will learn that *agape* love (divine love; wanting what is best for the other) purifies *erotic* love (wanting to be close to one's beloved).

Here are the analogies we use in the program:

Eros and *agape* in balance is like a cooling fan on a hot summer day, spreading air outward, refreshing all. *Eros* and *agape* imbalanced, however, is like a giant vacuum cleaner that pulls everything inward to itself. Signs of an imbalance—which is ultimately the nature of lust—include constantly texting, calling, instant messaging, and using social networks without restraint. These

> *"Love, to be real, must cost—it must hurt—it must empty us of self."*
> – St. Teresa of Calcutta (Mother Teresa)

are "red flags" signaling that someone may be acting more like a vacuum cleaner than a refreshing fan. Pope Benedict compares such relationships to a destructive drug.

Pornography, "Sexting," Fornication, and "How Far is Too Far?"

In brief, here are a few highlights of the chapter discussion of these issues:

- **Pornography**: Distorts, mocks, and hides the dignity of each person involved. It is a way of using people, the opposite of love. Science has shown that pornography changes the brain; thus, not only is the heart damaged, but the brain as well.[14]

- **"Sexting"**: Immodest pictures, lustful messages, or sexual conversations on phones or computers denigrate God's design for true love. When people share "sexts," they present themselves as objects to be used, with emotional hurt as a consequence. And because photos can also be retrieved years later (for instance, by college administrators or prospective employers who perform an Internet background check), the painful consequences can stretch far into the future.

- **Fornication**: Some middle schoolers may say, "How can this be wrong when we love each other?" The answer is this: before marriage, the only way to truthfully say, "I love you" with the language of the body is to save sexual activity for marriage. Otherwise, sex lies by "communicating" a lifelong, committed relationship that does not yet exist. Those who say, "I love you, so let's do this" are telling a lie both with words and actions. As a lie about love in this circumstance, sex is nothing more than *using another*.

- **How far is too far?** This common question can be addressed by the language of the body. Some actions speak the language of marital love, but since middle schoolers are not married, such actions constitute *use*, not love, and thus are "too far" when:

- ◦ The language of our bodies becomes sexually suggestive.
- ◦ Your behavior tempts one to lust or sin.
- ◦ You are thinking about how far you can get.
- ◦ Your body is becoming aroused.
- ◦ You are touching private body parts on someone else.
- ◦ You are making people around you uncomfortable.
- ◦ Your behavior is focused on stimulation.
- ◦ You are doing something you would not do in the presence of your parents.

The discussion of these topics is focused on pursuing the beauty of God's design, rather than on fear of negative consequences. Unfortunately, many young people have bought the lie. Thus, forgiveness is emphasized throughout the chapter. The sacrament of reconciliation (as well as counseling for those battling an addiction to something, such as pornography) is of the utmost importance.

Remember to pray for your child.

Prayer for Your Child

> *Dear God, Father, Son, and Holy Spirit,*
> *You have given us* [name of your child], *and we are called to love and care for him/her with our whole body and soul. Help us to show* [name of your child] *who he/she truly is in you! May the Theology of the Body guide us faithfully as a family. Amen.*

"To Use or Not to Use" Prayer for Your Child(ren)

Dear Jesus, Our Bridegroom, you would never use us. Please give strength to [name of your child] *to learn and live what it means to love and not use others. Amen.*

Questions for Your Middle Schooler:

1. I know you learned that the opposite of love is use. How do you think adults sometimes use kids? How do kids sometimes use adults?
2. What did you think about what you learned about *agape* and *eros*? Does it make sense to you? How does a couple learn to balance the two?
3. "Sexting" is such a violation because it takes that which is sacred and degrades it. What should you do when someone "sexts" you?
4. Statistics show that most teens have run across pornography. I know this is a sensitive subject, but know that you can be honest with me. Have you ever seen pornography? Is it something your friends struggle with? Do you struggle with it?

FAMILY APPLICATION:

1. **Billboard Sightings:** When you drive around with your child, be aware of the billboards that offer "counterfeit" sexual messages—messages that "counter" or subvert God's great plan for our sexuality. If you notice your child already seeing these images, talk to him or her about why it is counterfeit and how it is pornographic.

2. **Intentional Technology Protection Plan:** Tell your child that you care so much about him or her that you will randomly check his or her cell phone and computer. Discuss why you would do that. Have your child put him- or herself in your situation and ask what he or she would do. In addition, we highly recommend that you install internet filters on every desktop and laptop computer at your home. A few filter programs we recommend can be found at netnanny.com, cybersitter.com, and bsafehome.com. We also encourage you to consider obtaining spy software, which will help you to monitor or record activity on a network of computers. This is not an invasion of privacy. This is smart and responsible parenting (see spysoftware.com or spectorsoft.com).

3. **Midnight Snack-Chat:** Every now and then, allow your child to stay up late with you for a midnight snack. As you enjoy his or her favorite snack food, tell him or her a bit about you and your spouse: how you met; what your feelings were; what you did with such feelings; what loving things you did for each other; your engagement; your wedding; your first year; your joy at having him or her. If it goes well, it may become a ritual he or she requests, a code from your child to you, which really means, "Can we chat about some relationship stuff?"

RECOMMENDATIONS FOR FURTHER STUDY

For your child:

- *The Theology of His Body/Her Body* by Jason Evert

- *Pure of Heart: Breaking Free from Porn* by Jason Evert

For your own study:

- *The Great Divorce* by C.S. Lewis

- *The Violation of the Feminine* by Monica Ashour

- TheKingsMen.org *(an organization offering retreats and support groups for men to move from pornography into purity)*

Chapter Seven

Vocation

God's Call, My Response

Consider the implications of this true story. In the grocery store with her mother, a little six- or seven-year-old girl stared openly at a nun who was also shopping. The nun belonged to the community of the Nashville Dominicans, and she was dressed in the order's floor-length, beautiful, white habit. With a bright smile and delightful enthusiasm, the little girl said to her mother, "Mommy, she's getting married!"

Out of the mouths of babes! A consecrated sister or nun indeed symbolizes for all members of the Church that we are "brides" of Christ, the eternal Bridegroom, in the sense that we are all called to eternal union with God. The little girl in the grocery story captured precisely what the Church has taught throughout the ages and what St. John Paul II emphasizes in the Theology of the Body: "celibacy for the kingdom." We often use the term *vocation* ("to be called") exclusively in reference to the priesthood and religious life, but your son or daughter will learn that there is a universal call to holiness, as well as the vocations to marriage, consecrated life, and the priesthood. He or she will also learn to do the following:

> *"Every vocation, every path to which Christ calls us, ultimately leads to fulfillment and happiness, because it leads to God, to sharing God's own life." – John Paul II*

- Identify flaws in the secular understanding of dating.

- Consider how to live the universal call to holiness in daily life.

- Prepare for his or her future vocations by learning the significance of discernment.

"I Am Yours; You Are Mine": Matrimony and the "Zinger" of Marriage

Our union with God begins at our baptism, when we are grafted onto Christ, as part of his Mystical Body, the Church. Your child will learn that growing in holiness entails the call to be the best son or daughter, sibling, student, and friend he or she can be here and now. Responding to the call to holiness *now* prepares him or her for the future specific vocation God offers.

Union between a husband and wife in all areas of married life—from daily prayer to diaper-changing to dishes—shows forth the wonder of Jesus' total gift of himself on the cross and the Church's acceptance of that gift. For your child, we speak about the binding covenant to love and openness to life that the couple makes on the altar at their wedding.

St. John Paul II offers another beautiful insight, which is not elaborated upon in the chapter of the Student Workbook, but one that is useful for your own meditation. Conjugal love is the ultimate renewal of a couple's wedding vows. When a married couple unites in the marital embrace—freely, totally, faithfully, and fruitfully—they are, in a sense, participating in a liturgical act. Intercourse is a way of worshipping God! The Church does not disdain sex as a "necessary evil" for reproduction; rather, sex is so good, so sublime and sacred, that it is to be reserved for matrimony. The boundaries of sexual morality (i.e., as seen in the immorality of pornography, masturbation, extramarital sex, contraception, in vitro fertilization, cohabitation, etc.) are not irrelevant restrictions imposed by an outdated Church. No, they seek to preserve the actual truth, integrity, and sacredness of conjugal life and love.

"I am Yours; You Are Mine": Consecrated and Ordained Life

Our society today equates sex with love, so celibates (i.e., those who willingly forego marriage for the sake of Christ and the Church) are often seen as people who miss out on "love." On the contrary, they direct their total self to union with Christ and His Church and in a concrete way through Eucharistic union at Mass. John Paul II points out that every celibate is called to be fruitful, and the spiritual children of priests and religious are numerous. No wonder a priest is called "father" and consecrated women are called "sisters." Because they do not commit themselves exclusively to one person, they show the love of God is all-inclusive.

> *"Amen I say to you, 'there is no one who has given up house or brothers or sisters or mother or father or children or lands for my sake and for the sake of the gospel who will not receive a hundred times more now in present age ... " –*
> *Mark 10:29-30 (NAB)*

What we tell your child is "Be not afraid." God would *never* call us to a life of being miserable. Rather, our true vocation is the context within which we will most joyfully, peacefully, and successfully meet the trials of life with holiness. God did not intend for us to experience happiness *in spite* of our vocations, but *through* our vocations. The priest or religious who lives his or her vocation in true freedom should be joyful, lighthearted, and happy.

Remember to pray for your child.

Prayer for Your Child

Dear God, Father, Son, and Holy Spirit,
You have given us [name of your child], *and we are called to love and care for him/her with our whole body and soul. Help us to show* [name of your child] *who he/she truly is in you!*
May the Theology of the Body guide us faithfully as a family.
Amen.

"Vocation" Prayer for Your Child

*Dear Mother Mary and St. Joseph, you who lived both
celibacy and marriage, help [name of your child] to be open
to God's call. Amen.*

Questions for Your Middle Schooler:

1. Why do you think it is good to have priests around? What
    about sisters and nuns? (By the way, there is a slight
    difference between the two: *nuns* are cloistered, i.e.,
    they do not leave their convent, and they devote their
    lives to prayer; *religious sisters*, on the other hand, do
    active ministry work outside their convent.)
2. God calls each of us to a specific vocation. What are your
    thoughts about which vocation you might be called to?
3. Of all the priests and sisters you know, who seems the
    happiest? Why do you think that is?

FAMILY APPLICATION:

1. **Magnify the "Five L's":** Make a poster or carve a large piece of wood with a large letter L in it. Then, write **LOOK** (for the face of Christ). **LISTEN** (to the voice of Christ). **LEARN** (your purpose in life). **LIVE** (it to the max). **LOVE** (like God). Display this design in a prominent location and discuss the ideas with your child, encouraging him or her to discern in prayer daily what God wants. (These 5 L's of daily discernment are in your child's Student Workbook).

2. **Dinner Witness:** Invite both a priest and a consecrated religious to dinner, maybe separately. Ask them to share their vocation stories and enjoy being with them to let their joy and normalcy show forth.

3. **Normalize the Extraordinary:** Take your child to visit a nearby convent, monastery, or seminary. Spending time with good people in various vocations makes young people comfortable with the idea that God will one day call them to their vocation, maybe an extraordinary one. But it is hard to be open to something that is never seen or experienced!

RECOMMENDATIONS FOR FURTHER STUDY

For your child:

- *Mystery Trip LIVE,* a feature-length documentary available through a dynamic, live event format. DumbOxMinistries.com/mysterytrip
- "Five L's" – available at DumbOxMinistries.com

For your own personal growth:

- *Theology of the Body for Beginners* by Christopher West
- *What Does God Want? A Practical Guide to Making Decisions* by Fr. Michael Scanlon
- *The Meaning of Vocation* by St. John Paul II

Chapter
Eight

Hope and Future
Daily Living Out the Language of the Body

Tick. Tick. Tick. Can you hear the time bomb? "A time bomb about to go off" is the metaphor used for the life-changing explosion that the Theology of the Body will make in those who live it in truth, according George Weigel, the official biographer of Pope John Paul II.

Setting off this "TOB time bomb" means that radical change can happen in young people, enabling them to reject secularism and to embrace life in Christ by living the language of the body. This undertaking has been our hope and prayer. This last chapter summarizes and revisits ideas learned throughout the program and reminds middle schoolers to do the following:

- Trust in God's plan for their futures.

- Embrace their baptismal promises in a living relationship with Jesus Christ.

- Use their bodies to "speak" truth.

- Apply core concepts of the Theology of the Body to the following:
  ◦ Friends: bullying, gossip, peer pressure, social justice.
  ◦ Family: broken or dysfunctional, lack of intimacy with parents, siblings.
  ◦ World: the Corporal Works of Mercy, social justice.

- Overcome fear and make a deeper commitment to embrace and live their Catholic faith.

Not Co-incident but God-incident

Two of the authors, Colin and Aimee MacIver, once attended a youth conference at which chastity pledge cards were offered. They both signed their own cards and kept them. The amazing "God-incident" is that—even though they didn't know each other at the time and lived in different states—they realized after they were married and sorting through memorabilia that they had attended the same conference and signed the same card on the same date!

It is not a coincidence that you are your child's parent. It is not a co-incidence that your child is in this program. It is not a coincidence that you are reading this Parent's Guide. God wants what is best for your family. As we emphasize to your child the daily living out of life in Christ, we reiterate the same message for you and for us as well: **none** of this is possible without grace (the eternal exchange of life and love between the Father, Son, and Holy Spirit). And the truth will not take root without you being a model and mentor to your child. Your life of intimacy with Christ through prayer, the sacraments, and virtue will make the time bomb a real explosion—an explosion of Love.

> *"Young people: Enter into a personal dialogue with Jesus Christ and cultivate it in faith. Get to know him better by reading the Gospels and the* Catechism of the Catholic Church.*"*
> – *Pope Benedict XVI*

Summary for Sanctity: Major Themes Given to Your Child

Union with God: We started with the analogy of a map, and now we reiterate it for your middle schooler. Our faith and our bodies have everything to do with each other. The spiritual world is made visible through the sacraments. The person being baptized can feel the water and know he is being cleansed of sin. We can see and taste Jesus' body and blood, knowing that is the most intimate union with God ever on earth.

Union With Others:

- **Friends** – But God wants us in relationship not only with him but with others. Your child has been taught that true friends want the best for the other. Friends are like teammates on a gold-medal team, encouraging each other as well as challenging each other, especially during tough games. The same is true for the game of life. "Friends" who are destructive and tear you down (through bullying; cyber bullying; gossiping; texting, rather than listening; drinking; disobeying parents; and bad partying) are not true teammates.

- **Family** – The family is a "school of love," a place of unconditional love. True love entails sacrificing for each other (listening to your sister; playing with your little brother; helping your mom make dinner; asking your dad about his work; apologizing for mistakes; and forgiving one another, etc.). No family is perfect, but security is given by unconditional love.

- **Friends-to-Be** – We are called to help others. Jesus spoke the truth of the language of his body by healing people, multiplying bread, and forgiving others. You too should reach out to the "least of your brethren" through the corporal works of mercy: feed the hungry; give drink to the thirsty; shelter the homeless; care for the sick; visit the imprisoned; clothe the naked; and bury the dead. By serving others, you don't just help them; you grow closer to Jesus.

Union Within Oneself:

The body should speak the truth. Chastity means living the truth of the language of our bodies—with a pure heart and pure bodily actions—by not using others through our sexuality, but by loving everyone we encounter. Chastity includes modest clothes; wholesome entertainment (whether it be via TV, movies, music, games, etc.); speaking; texting; emailing; and using social networks with respect and purity. Chastity does not flow from a checklist but from a pure heart.

"Be Not Afraid ... To Give Them Better"

Your child deserves a better understanding of his or her sexuality than what the world is offering. Pope Benedict XVI recently said, "Children deserve to grow up with a healthy understanding of sexuality and its proper place in human relationships. They should be spared the degrading manifestations and the crude manipulation of sexuality so prevalent today. They have a right to be educated in authentic moral values rooted in the dignity of the human person."[15] The Theology of the Body is just such an education in human dignity. It is a challenge to keep the lead role in your child's life, but *be not afraid!* We tell your middle schooler that these words are the ones most repeated in the New Testament, and they were reiterated time and again by St. John Paul II.

Your task of raising your child is formidable. Be not afraid! You may have made wrong decisions in your past. You may not fully understand all that is being presented here. You may be humbled by the task of forming your child against the secularism running rampant. Be not afraid!

Ask Jesus to guide you as a person and as a parent. We can trust the words of him who died for love of us: "Do not let your hearts be troubled... I am the way and the truth and the life ... Get up, let us go" (John 14:1, 6, 31, NAB).

> *"And is not the enraptured gaze of Mary as she contemplated the face of the newborn Christ and cradled him in her arms that unparalleled model of love which should inspire us every time we receive Eucharistic communion?"*
> – *Pope John Paul II,*
> **The Eucharist and its Relationship to the Church, 55**

Remember to pray for your child.

Prayer for Your Child

Dear God, Father, Son, and Holy Spirit,
You have given us [name of your child], *and we are called to*
love and care for him/her with our whole body and soul. Help
us to show [name of your child] *who he/she truly is in you!*
May the Theology of the Body guide us faithfully as a family.
Amen.

"Hope and Future" Prayer for Your Child

Dear Jesus, You promised abundant life to us. I pray for
my child and ask that you give him/her the strength to live
according to the teachings of the gospel as seen through the
Theology of the Body, so that he/she might have abundant
life not only here on earth, but eternally with you, the Father,
and the Holy Spirit, and all the angels and saints in heaven.
Amen.

Questions for Your Middle Schooler:

1. Do you know someone who has experienced cyber-bullying? What did he or she do about it? Why do you think people bully others?
2. Are you excited, scared, or anxious about your future? Who do you want to be when you grow up?
3. Which of your friends do you think you will be friends with for life? Why? How do you try to be a good friend to your peers?

FAMILY APPLICATION:

1. **Heart-to-Heart:** Have a "Heart to Heart" night or outing. Discuss the following questions: "When I think about the future, I wonder about … I am scared of … I am excited about … "

2. **Corporal Calendar:** Decide on which corporal work of mercy you will do as a family. Put it down on your calendar as a monthly event. After visiting the sick or the imprisoned (etc.), share with each other what was most profound for you. What did you notice? How were *you* changed?

3. **Visual Spiritual Diary:** Go through pictures of your child's baptism and First Holy Communion. Tell about your hopes and dreams you had then and that you have now for him or her. Talk seriously about what your baptism and First Holy Communion means to you, and discuss how the whole family can work to live out the power of baptism and the union given at Mass.

RECOMMENDATIONS FOR FURTHER STUDY

For your child:

- *Pure Faith: A Prayer Book for Teens* by Jason Evert
- *Purity 365: Daily Reflections on Purity* by Jason Evert

For your own personal growth:

- *Social Networking: How to Plug in Without Tuning Out* by Monica Ashour
- *Heaven: The Heart's Deepest Longing* by Peter Kreeft
- *The Heart of the World* by Hans Urs Von Balthasar
- The Pontifical Council for the Family. *The Truth and Meaning of Human Sexuality: Guidelines for Education within the Family*

Notes

1 MacArthur Foundation Research Network on Adolescent Development and Juvenile Justice: Less Guilty by Reason of Adolescence (Issue Brief #3), Temple University, Department of Psychology, www.adjj.org
2 National Institute of Mental Health. "Teenage Brain: A Work in Progress" (Fact Sheet), http://www.nimh.nih.gov/health/publications/teenage-brain-a-work-in-progress-fact-sheet/index.shtml [Accessed March 31, 2011.]
3 Ibid.
4 Gardner, M., & Steinberg, L. (2005). Peer influence on risk-taking, risk preference, and risky decision-making in adolescence and adulthood: An experimental study. *Developmental Psychology*, 41, 625-635.
5 The Pontifical Council for the Family. *The Truth and Meaning of Human Sexuality: Guidelines for Education within the Family.* (Boston: Pauline Books and Media, 1996), no. 115.
6 Ibid, 5.
7 Ibid, 134.
8 Pope Benedict XVI. *To Look on Christ: Exercises in Faith, Hope, and Love* (New York: Crossroads, 1991).
9 Ibid, 134.
10 Hans Urs von Balthasar. "Movement toward God." *Explorations in Theology*, vol. 3, 15-55.
11 *Gaudium et Spes,* no. 22.

12 *The Truth and Meaning of Human Sexuality*: "Only information
    proportionate to each phase of their individual development
    should be presented to children and young people," no. 124.
13 TOB 57:2-3; 126:4. (*Pietas* is the key gift of the Holy Spirit in the
    spirituality of marriage, according to *Humanae Vitae,* no. 131:2-6).
14 *The Social Costs of Pornography: A Collection of Papers*
    (Princeton, N.J.: Witherspoon Institute, 2010); see also N.
    Doidge, *The Brain that Changes Itself: Stories of Personal
    Triumph from the Frontiers of Brain Science* (New York: Viking,
    2007).
15 Pope Benedict XVI, "Address to U.S. Bishops, National Shrine of
    the Immaculate Conception in Washington, D.C.," April 16, 2008